Indonesia

Robin Lim

✿ Carolrhoda Books, Inc. / Minneapolis

Photo Acknowledgments

Photographs, maps, and artworks are used courtesy of: John Erste, pp. 1, 2–3, 8–9, 16, 20–21, 24–25, 32–33, 35, 41; Laura Westlund, pp. 4–5, 11, 25 (bottom); © Trip/C.C., pp. 6, 37, 39 (bottom), 40 (left); © Trip/ R. Nichols, pp. 7, 27 (top); © Trip/W. Jacobs, p. 8; © Trip/P. Mercea, pp. 9, 13 (right), 40 (right); © Eugene G. Schulz, pp. 10 (left), 20; © Michele Burgess, pp. 10 (right), 12, 14, 16, 17, 18, 26, 30 (top), 33 (left), 36, 38, 43 (left); © Trip/T. Knight, pp. 11, 13 (left); © Trip/A. Tovy, pp. 15 (left), 27 (bottom), 30 (bottom); © Trip/J. Sweeney, p. 15 (right); © Trip/Trip, pp.19, 31 (bottom); © Trip/T. Lester, p. 21 (top); © Trip/D. Clegg, pp. 21 (bottom), 22 (both), 23 (bottom), 32; © Trip/J. Lamb, p. 23 (top); © Betty Crowell, pp. 28, 42; © Trip/J. Pugh, pp. 29, 35; © Trip/T. Bognar, p. 31 (top); © Trip/M. Nichols, p. 33 (right); © Trip/L. Clark, p. 34; © Trip/M. Both, p. 39 (top); © Trip/G. Grieves, p. 43 (right); © Trip/J. Wakelin, p. 44. Cover photograph of Javanese puppets courtesy of © Trip/R. Nicols.

Carolrhoda Books, Inc.
A division of Lerner Publishing Group
241 First Avenue North
Minneapolis, MN 55401 U.S.A.

Website address: www.lernerbooks.com

Words in **bold type** are explained in a glossary that begins on page 44.

Library of Congress Cataloging-in-Publication Data

Lim, Robin, 1956–
    Indonesia / Robin Lim.
        p. cm. — (Globe-trotter's club)
    Includes index.
    Summary: Examines the culture, language, and history of Indonesia.
    ISBN 1-57505-150-8 (lib. bdg. : alk. paper)
        1. Indonesia—Juvenile literature. [1. Indonesia.] I. Title.
II. Globe-trotters club (Series)
DS615.L54 2001
959.8—dc21
                                                                                00–008034

Manufactured in the United States of America
1 2 3 4 5 6 – JR – 06 05 04 03 02 01

Contents

Selamat Datang ke **Indonesia!***

*That's "Welcome to Indonesia" in Bahasa Indonesia, the official language of Indonesia.

You will find the country of Indonesia, the world's largest **archipelago,** north of Australia and south of the **continent** of Asia. Indonesia consists of 13,677 islands. The major islands of Indonesia are Sumatra, Java, West Timor, Flores, Bali, Celebes, Borneo, and half of New Guinea.

ASIA

S U L U
SEA

Medan

M A L A Y S I A

CELEBES

SEA

KALIMANTAN
PROVINCE
(BORNEO)

G R E A T E R   S U N D A   I S L A N D S

S U M A T R A

BARISAN MTNS.

I N D O N E S I A

SULAWESI
(CELEBES)

J A V A
SEA

Jakarta

MADURA

FLORES

BALI
SEA

KOMODO   Larantuka

Miles

0   100   200   300

0   200   400

Kilometers

J A V A

BALI   LOMBOK

SUMBAWA

FLORES

SUMBA

N

INDIAN OCEAN

LESSER SUNDA

Water, water, and more water! The Pacific Ocean lies to the northeast of Indonesia. The Indian Ocean washes the islands in the south. The Arafura Sea separates Indonesia from Australia in the southeast. The Java Sea lies north of Java. You'll find the Bali Sea to the north of Bali. The Flores Sea laps against the northern side of Flores and the Lesser Sunda Islands. The Timor Sea floats between Timor and Australia. The Celebes Sea and the Sulu Sea separate Indonesia from the Philippines.

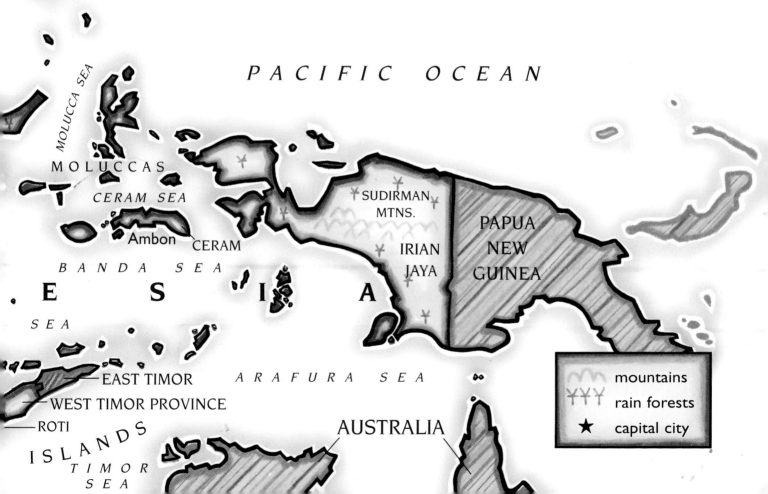

PHILIPPINES

PACIFIC OCEAN

MOLUCCA SEA

MOLUCCAS

CERAM SEA

Ambon CERAM

BANDA SEA

E   S   I   A

SUDIRMAN MTNS.

IRIAN JAYA

PAPUA NEW GUINEA

SEA

EAST TIMOR

WEST TIMOR PROVINCE

ROTI

ISLANDS

TIMOR SEA

ARAFURA SEA

AUSTRALIA

⌇⌇	mountains
⅄⅄⅄	rain forests
★	capital city

Indonesia is covered with green farmland and rain forests. This lush valley is on Sulawesi Island.

Island
Hopping

Indonesia is made up of four island chains—the Greater Sunda Islands, the Lesser Sunda Islands, the Molucca Islands, and Irian Jaya.

The Greater Sunda Islands include Sumatra and Java. Sumatra's eastern side is covered with forests and swamps. The Barisan Mountain range dominates the island's western coast. Java is the most populated island and home of the nation's capital, Jakarta.

Fast Facts about Indonesia

Name: Republic of Indonesia
Area: 741,101 square miles
Main Landforms: Maoke Mountains, Barisan Mountains, Muller Mountains, Schwaner Mountains, Lake Toba
Major Rivers: Barito River, Kapuas River
Highest Point: Mount Java (16,499 feet)
Lowest Point: Sea level
Animals: Silvery gibbon, tarsier, Sulawesi civet cat, Komodo dragon
Capital City: Jakarta
Other Major Cities: Surabaya, Medan, Bandung, Semarang
Official Language: Bahasa Indonesia
Money Unit: Rupiah

Bali, with **volcanoes** and a vast central plain, is an island in the Lesser Sunda chain. Lombok, Sumbawa, Sumba, Flores, and Timor are also part of the Lesser Sundas. Flores is a small rugged island with 14 active volcanoes.

The Moluccas are a collection of old volcanoes. **Tropical rain forests,** rugged mountains, coral gardens, and deserted beaches dot the Moluccas. Irian Jaya, on Indonesia's easternmost island, is the most sparsely populated. Irian Jaya is rich with copper and gold mines.

Tropical rain forests are warm, wet, and very green.

How's the Weather?

The islands of Indonesia spread across the **equator,** an imaginary line that circles the center of the earth. The sun's rays shine intensely on the equator, pushing temperatures above the 80-degree mark for much of the year. This kind of climate is called tropical. Plants of all kinds thrive in the heat.

Very little rain falls between the months of May and September, Indonesia's dry season. But from October through April, Indonesia has a wet season. In some parts of the country, this means a pleasant afternoon downfall. In Maluku and in the rain forests, however, rain can fall for weeks without a break.

Indonesian farmers have created these terraces for farming. Can you see the volcano in the distance?

Quaking in
Your Boots

Use your finger to trace an imaginary circle on a globe. Start in Indonesia and arc north through the Philippines and Japan. Then head east to brush the tip of the Russian Federation and Alaska. Move south along the coast of Canada, the United States, Mexico, Central America, and South America. Swing westward to catch New Zealand and return to Indonesia. Within this circle—which geologists call the Ring of Fire— you'll find most of the world's volcanoes and **earthquakes.**

The earth's surface, called the crust, is like a giant puzzle. The puzzle pieces are huge slabs called **tectonic plates.** These plates move and grind against each other, causing earthquakes. Sometimes when plates collide, one sinks be-

create giant water waves called tidal waves, or *tsunamis.*

Making Islands

In 1883 the island of Krakatoa, located between Java and Sumatra, exploded in a volcanic blast. The eruption caused massive tidal waves and shot tons of volcanic ash miles into the sky. The explosion was heard 2,400 miles away in Alice Springs, Australia. In 1925 a new island, Anak Krakatoa (which means "Child of Krakatoa"), appeared above the ocean's surface. Since then it has risen and submerged five times.

Volcanic eruptions can cover nearby cities in tons of ash or engulf cars and buildings in hot lava.

low the other and begins to melt. The melted rock, called magma, forces its way up between two plates to create a volcano. Modern-day Indonesia is home to more than 125 active volcanoes.

9

Flowers of all colors bloom in Indonesia. Buy a bouquet or two at the flower market in Jakarta (left). Development on Sumatra Island has made it hard for the Sumatran tiger to find food (below).

Critters
Undercover

More than 35,000 different kinds of plants grow in Indonesia. Kalimantan, the Indonesian part of the island of Borneo, has more than 800 varieties of orchids and more than 1,100 different kinds of ferns. The world's biggest bloom, the rafflesia arnoldi, grows on the island of Sumatra. Indonesia's most useful plant is the kelapa, also known as a coconut palm. You can drink the water from the young green coconut to quench your thirst or to soothe a stomachache. Indonesians use kelapa wood to build houses, make furniture, and create sculpture.

Among the lush foliage live lots of animals. On Sumatra, rhinoceroses, orangutans, Sumatran tigers, tapirs,

Dear Grandpa,
Yesterday was so fun! We took a ferry from Labuhanbajo, Flores, to the island of Komodo to see the dragons. Wow! Komodo dragons have scales and can grow to be more than 12 feet long. They use their tongues to smell. Our tour guide told us that the dragons flick their forked tongues to sniff out their prey. Komodo dragons have more than 60 very sharp teeth. I wanted to take one home, but mom said, "No way." *Selamat jalan!* (That's Bahasa Indonesia for "happy travels.")

—Josh

sunbears, flying foxes, slow loris, barking mouse deer, elephants, and goat antelopes all roam free. The world's largest known butterfly, with a wingspan as wide as 11 inches, is Indonesia's Queen Alexandra's Bird-wing. The males have metallic blue, black, and green markings on their wings. The females are less colorful and bigger. These butterflies are so big they actually soar through the treetops like birds in flight.

One Big Bloom

The rafflesia arnoldi is a fungus that lives on the roots of a jungle vine. A brown, cabbage-sized bud pushes through rotting leaves. Nine months later, the bud opens into a huge red or orange flower with white spots. The bloom's putrid smell—similar to rotting meat—attracts flies. Then the plant eats the tasty flies.

People in Indonesia have grown rice for thousands of years.

First **People**

In 2000 B.C., ancestors of the modern Malay people began to migrate to Indonesia. Over the course of many, many generations, the newcomers settled on the coasts. They built wooden houses, wove their own cloth, and made pottery. They used stone tools and grew rice. Another wave of Malay immigrants arrived on the Indonesian islands around the year 250 B.C. They also settled along the coasts, pushing previous inhabitants farther inland. This group used bronze tools and survived on the rice they grew and the plants they found.

Indian traders introduced Indonesians to Hinduism and Buddhism in the A.D. 100s. Indian culture seeped into the islands. Indonesians even based their written language on a form of the Indian Sanskrit alphabet. Eventually, the Melanesians also migrated from the continent of Australia to the easternmost islands of the Indonesian archipelago.

Indonesians weave patterned cloth on a loom (above). **These young Indonesians** (above right) **are making colorful pottery much like their ancestors did.**

Java Man

In 1891 a Dutch doctor named Eugene Dubois unearthed a skull while working in central Java. The skull had a low brow and prominent jaw. It belonged to Java Man, an ancestor of humans, who lived 500,000 years ago.

Since Dr. Dubois found Java Man, scientists have uncovered even older bones. The finds include a child's skull that may be as many as 1.98 million years old.

Many **Are One**

 Indonesia's national motto is "Bhinneka Tunggal Ika," which in old Javanese means "They are many, they are one." Would you believe that Indonesia has approximately 300 different **ethnic groups**? The members of these ethnic groups live in separate areas of Indonesia.

The Javanese have settled in the central and eastern parts of Java. The Sundanese live in west Java. Many Madurese reside in east Java. The Madurese are originally from Madura, an island off of Java's northeast coast.

On Sumatra, the nomadic Kubu live in the dense jungle and swamps along the eastern coast. The Kubu

This Sundanese man and his daughter carry their coconuts to sell at the market.

Kids from Bali (left) **seem happy to be sporting their Garfield and Popeye T-shirts.**

are descendants of the first Malay people to settle in Indonesia. The Batak make their homes in the fertile valleys of northern Sumatra, where they grow rice and weave amazing cloth.

Flores has five main languages and ethnic groups—the Manggarai, the Ngada, the Ende, and their close relatives, the Lio. The Lamaholot call Larantuka home.

The Yali girls above live on Irian Jaya. Their ancestors were Aboriginal Australians.

Up **North**

Folks make their homes in the Northern Islands, too. In Kalimantan the Malay-Indonesian people live along the coasts. The Dayaks live in the mountains. They craft earthenware pottery, bone ornaments, stone tools, and handwoven cotton textiles.

The Toraja live in the mountains on the island of Sulawesi. The Toraja are ethnically unlike the other people of Sulawesi. Some

This Torajan girl wears a ricing hat to keep the heat of the sun at bay while farming her family's lands.

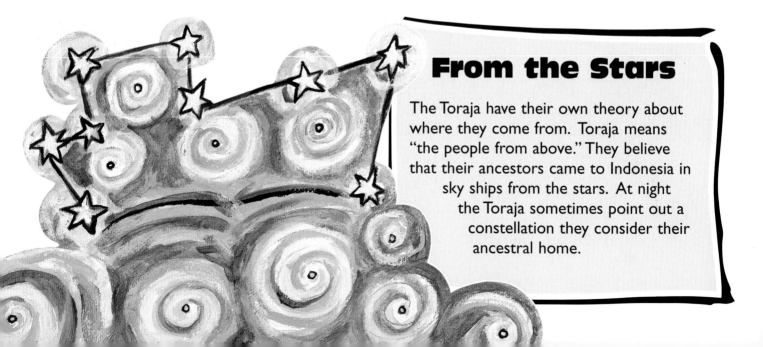

From the Stars

The Toraja have their own theory about where they come from. Toraja means "the people from above." They believe that their ancestors came to Indonesia in sky ships from the stars. At night the Toraja sometimes point out a constellation they consider their ancestral home.

scientists believe the Toraja sailed from Cambodia and were blown to Indonesia by a storm.

About 1.5 million people live in the Molucca Islands. The Alfuro people are related to Aboriginal Australians, who live in the Australian Outback. The Ambonese, a Malay people, live along the coasts and around the city of Ambon.

Some Papuans live in the high valleys and plateaus of Irian Jaya. Other Papuans live in the coastal and foothill areas of the island. Pygmy people live in extreme isolation on the island's rough Sudirman Mountain range. The Asmat people dwell on Irian Jaya's southern coast.

These Dayak women live in eastern Kalimantan on the island of Borneo.

Family Ties

In Indonesia's small villages, many children live with their parents, brothers, sisters, grandparents, aunts, uncles, and cousins. This is known as a *keluarga adat*, or **extended family.** All the grown-ups take turns looking after the young ones.

Babies and small children sleep with their parents or grandparents. Some people have a mattress on their bed platform. Others have a tikar, a woven mat spread out to cover a raised platform. Tikars are nice and cool on warm nights.

Family life in Indonesia is different in the cities, where children live with their parents, siblings, and sometimes a grandparent. Even with this difference, some traditions are the same in both parts of Indonesia. In the cities and in the countryside, whoever is older is always right! Because parents and grandparents have lived longer and know more about life, they expect their kids and grandkids to respect them.

Indonesians might live with their extended families in a traditional house like this one in Kete Kesu on Sulawesi.

18

This Indonesian family lives in a city, without their extended family in their home.

All in the Family

Here are the Bahasa Indonesia words for family members. Practice using these terms on your own family. See if they can understand you!

grandfather	*kakek*	kah-KEHK
grandmother	*nenek*	neh-NEHK
father	*ayah*	EYE-yah
mother	*ibu*	EE-boo
uncle	*paman*	pah-MAHN
aunt	*bibi*	BEE-bee
son	*anak lalaki*	AH-nahk lah-lah-KEE
daughter	*anak prempuan*	AH-nahk prehm-PWAHN
younger brother or sister	*adik*	AH-dihk
older brother or sister	*kakak*	kah-KAHK

Take a ride around the big city of Jakarta in a three-wheeled taxi!

Jam-packed **Cities**

Indonesia's cities are crowded and noisy. Getting around cities, such as Jakarta, can be a challenge. Taxis, cars, buses, horse-drawn carriages, and people jockey for room on narrow streets. A *bemo*, an open-air minibus, is one way to go. Be prepared, though. Bemo drivers are notorious for going very fast. It's common to see a bemo in the ditch, tipped over on its side. The passengers get out to help the driver put it back on the road. It can be scary, but the price is right. For 50 *rupiah* (about 2½ cents) a bemo will speed you across town. On motorbikes, called *speda* motors, people haul everything from dozens of eggs stacked on wire racks to couches and chairs.

In Jakarta, new office buildings, department stores, and hotels tower over the red-roofed homes built in the 1800s. Families living in an Indonesian city may live in a concrete house with a tile roof. Other city dwellers may live in wood and cardboard structures with corrugated tin roofs.

Jakarta (above) **is the most polluted city in the world. On very hot, humid days, a milky haze hangs over the city. To get out of the traffic, you can ride a pedicab** (right) **in the countryside.**

Life in the
Countryside

An ox helps these kids (left) **get out to the fields. This boy** (above) **on Lombok Island shows off his family's rice harvest.**

Life in the countryside is a bit slower. Most children wake up at dawn. For breakfast, their mother or grandmother cooks rice on a wood stove. The kids walk to school. After school many children work in their family's ricefields.

Most families in the countryside work on farms. Rice is the usual crop. Farmers use an oxen-pulled plow on the fields. Then men plant

brown rice, and even red rice.

rice seedlings in flooded fields called *sawahs*. For centuries Indonesian farmers have built terraces like shelves into the hills. They flood these terraces with water to help the rice grow.

Just before harvesttime, farmers open the floodgates to allow water to drain from the sawahs. When the fields dry, women cut and separate the grain from the plant. They spread the rice out in the sun to dry and then send the grain to a mill to be processed.

Farmers make watery rice terraces (above) **that take on the shapes of the surrounding landscape.**

Women thresh rice, or separate the seeds from the plants, by hand.

Time for Chores

What kinds of chores do you have to do at home? Kids who live in the Indonesian countryside help carve wooden handicrafts, paint, make grass roofs, feed the pigs, and pluck chickens.

To protect the crop from birds, families make scarecrows. Some people hang brightly colored plastic bags, bells, and tin pans on posts to scare away the birds. Kids run through the sawahs to shoo away the hungry birds.

Bahasa
Indonesia

People speak more than 365 languages in Indonesia. In an effort to unite the islands, the government made Bahasa Indonesia the nation's official language in 1945. Based on the Malay and Javanese languages, Bahasa Indonesia includes Dutch, Portuguese, and Arabic words, too. Bahasa Indonesia is the language Indonesian kids learn in school. To write a letter or report in Bahasa, Indonesian kids use the same alphabet that English speakers use.

At home, though, kids are likely to speak the language their parents grew up speaking. Most Indonesians can speak two or more languages.

Selamat siang

What's in a Name?

In Bali, Indonesia, it's very easy to remember first names. The Sudra people always use one of only four first names! Boy or girl, all first-born children are named Wayan. Second babies are named Made. The third child is Nyoman, and fourth children are named Ketut. At five, the names repeat. For example, a fifth brother or sister will be named Wayan, and so on.

Greet an Indonesian

Here are a few greetings in Bahasa Indonesia. Try them out on a friend!

blessings on your morning (early part of the day)	*selamat pagi*	(seh-lah-MAHT PAH-gee)
blessings on your midday (when the sun is high)	*selamat siang*	(seh-lah-MAHT see-ANG)
blessings on your late day (late afternoon to twilight)	*selamat sore*	(seh-lah-MAHT soh-RAY)
blessings on your night (after dark)	*selamat malam*	(seh-lah-MAHT mah-LAHM)
happy travels	*selamat jalan*	(seh-lah-MAHT jah-LAHN)
blessings on your sleep	*selamat tidur*	(seh-lah-MAHT tee-DOR)
sweet dreams	*mimpi manis*	(MIHM-pee MAHN-ihs)

The Indonesian flag represents a country with many islands and several ethnicities. The flag has been flown in Indonesia since 1945, when the country declared its independence from the Netherlands.

Religious **Beliefs**

In Indonesia there are only five legal religions—Agama Islam, Agama Hindu, Agama Christian Protestant, Agama Christian Katolik, and Agama Buddha.

About 88 percent of Indonesians are Muslim. Islam is the state religion. In all the major cities, Masjids (Arabic for mosques) broadcast the morning and evening call to prayer over a crackly loudspeaker. Activity stops as people face west, toward the holy city of Mecca, in Saudi Arabia, to pray. Muslims need not go to a mosque to worship—when they hear the call to prayer, the airport, the ricefield, the shopping mall, or any other place will do.

Some Indonesians are animists. Indonesians call the animistic beliefs Agama Asli. Asli means "real," and the animists represent the beliefs of those who first settled the islands. Animists believe that all natural things—including plants, animals, and objects such as rocks—have souls. Many Indonesians combine animist beliefs with other religions.

Muslims worship at mosques like Gang Bengkok Mosque in Medan on Sumatra Island.

Agama Hindu

Agama Hindu followers believe that the soul never dies. When bodies die, souls rest until being reborn. Most Balinese Hindu kids will tell you that they hope to be reborn into their same family when they die. Over time, a soul is believed to reach a state of consciousness that is at one with God.

On warm days, Borobudur Temple on Java Island (above) fills up with people. Worshipers sit outside beneath the colorful umbrellas and scarves (left) at Bangli Pura Kehen Temple on Bali Island.

Celebrate
Ramadan

Ramadan is the holiest time of year in Islam. Ramadan falls in the ninth month of the Javanese calendar. For the month's thirty days, adult Muslims fast (do not eat or drink) from sunrise to sunset.

In Indonesia during Ramadan, Muslim families get up before dawn and eat and drink as much as they can. At sunrise each village, town, or city has a public call to prayer. Muslim villagers pray together. All eating and drinking stops for the day.

Muslim women cover their heads with white scarves during Ramadan.

28

Muslim girls have a snack break during kindergarten.

As sunset approaches, hungry and thirsty people wait for the call to prayer. After they pray, everyone can eat.

The month of Ramadan ends with a community prayer. Men go to the front of the group, wearing black headpieces. Women, dressed in white, kneel in the back. To end the prayer, the whole group bows in unison and kisses the ground.

After Ramadan

The three days after Ramadan are called id al-Fitr. Families visit and share special sweet treats and dates. People ask each other for forgiveness for wrongs they have done during the previous year.

Kids at this school (left) **in eastern Kalimantan play games in the grass during recess. Gym class means uniforms for these kids on Lombok Island** (below). **Stand up straight!**

Going to
School

Put on that red and white uniform! It's time for school. The students arrive before the teachers to sweep the school grounds. In the dry season, students water plants and trees in the school's garden.

In Indonesia, grades one through six are called Sekola Dasar, or SD. Students study mathematics, reading, writing, history, government, religion, and social studies. In citizenship class, kids learn how to cooperate. So many SDs dot Indonesia that few kids have a long hike to school.

Junior high is called Sekola Menengah Pertama, and it lasts for three years. There are far fewer SMPs than SDs, so the children may have to walk much farther to school once they are in junior high.

Only about 25 percent of the kids who attend school in Indonesia

Hari Raya Saraswati

Each year Balinese children and their teachers celebrate Hari Raya Saraswati. Saraswati is the Hindu goddess of learning. On Saraswati's holy day, no one reads books, plays instruments, or uses computers. This is the day these things are blessed.

Kids get the day off from school. They wake up early, bathe, and put on their finest clothes. The girls carry small towers of fruit and cakes on their heads to the village school. They pray together in the schoolyard. Each child silently gives thanks to the goddess who watches over their education.

Don't drop the fruit! Women carry baskets on their heads to give to the Hindu goddess of learning.

graduate from high school. SMA (Sekola Menengah Atas)—high school—is too expensive for many families. Most SMA students are boys. Girls usually work at home or get jobs to help support their family.

Jakarta students pay attention in class. Who knows what will be on next week's English quiz?

Sarong **Along**

Anybody can wear a sarong! This Sasak boy from Lombok Island models his by a banana stand.

In Indonesia lots of people wear sarongs, a six-foot-long piece of fabric wrapped around the waist and tied. At night sarongs make great blankets.

Some sarongs are handwoven cotton ikat. Ikat can be as thick as denim. Weavers use brown, deep red, and dark blue thread to weave designs or pictures of birds, roses, or angels into the fabric. Other sarongs are made of silk. Weavers blend silk and cotton to make the endek sarongs that Hindus wear to temple in Bali.

The islanders of Java and Madura are famous for their fancy batik sarongs. To make batik, workers use wax to draw beautiful patterns on

32

Batik artists (left) **create beautiful cloth with designs made from hot wax. Ikat weavers like this one** (below) **create pretty patterns in dark-colored cloth.**

cloth. When the wax dries, the workers dip the fabric in dye. Then workers boil the cloth to remove the wax. Batik can be seen drying on the bushes and clotheslines of remote Indonesian villages.

Use Your **Hands**

On the islands of Java and Bali, people use *wayang kulit* (shadow puppets) to tell their tales. Late at night, the audience gathers to watch the show. Hidden from the view of the audience by a white screen, a *dalang* (puppeteer) controls the puppets and provides music by playing a small gamelan, or xylophone, with his feet. The plays are usually based on the Hindu epics the *Ramayana* or the *Mahabarata*. Puppeteers also include local **folktales** and fantastic stories of good versus evil. At the end of most stories, good triumphs over evil. Folktales often explain events in nature, such as how the world began.

The show lasts all night. As the first light of dawn appears on the horizon, the weary dalang ends the show. Parents carry their sleepy children home.

Brightly painted puppets are sold on village streets.

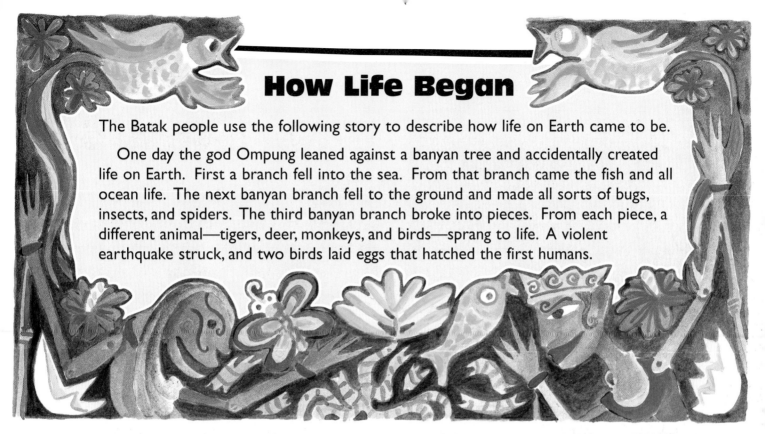

How Life Began

The Batak people use the following story to describe how life on Earth came to be.

One day the god Ompung leaned against a banyan tree and accidentally created life on Earth. First a branch fell into the sea. From that branch came the fish and all ocean life. The next banyan branch fell to the ground and made all sorts of bugs, insects, and spiders. The third banyan branch broke into pieces. From each piece, a different animal—tigers, deer, monkeys, and birds—sprang to life. A violent earthquake struck, and two birds laid eggs that hatched the first humans.

These puppets from Yokyakarta on Java Island wear detailed clothing and colorful carved masks. Puppet shows can last for hours.

Bamboo
Jamboree

Bamboo, a fast-growing grass that originated in Asia, grows like crazy all over Indonesia. Bamboo instruments play a big part in the country's folk music tradition. You will find bamboo flutes on nearly every island. Schoolchildren of the Moluccas carry their bamboo flutes with them wherever they go. The sad-sounding string instrument of Roti island, the *susando*, is made with a stalk of bamboo and a dried palm leaf and it is strung with wire. The

Children's bamboo bands keep up Indonesia's folk music tradition.

English can sing Beatles songs!

angklung of West Java is a series of bamboo tubes suspended from a frame. Musicians shake the tubes against the frame to create amazing music. The *gamelan joged bumbung* of Bali is an orchestra of bamboo xylophones.

In the Moluccas, two long bamboo poles are used in the *bambu gila* or "dangerous dance." Two dancers kneel at opposite ends of the poles, which they click together in time to the music. Other dancers step and jump between the poles as the music gets faster and faster.

These Benuaq dancers (above) **from eastern Kalimantan do the dances of their ancestors.**

Cicek-cicek/Gecko
(An Indonesian Children's Song)

Gecko, gecko on the wall	Cicek-cicek di dingding	CHEE-chuck CHEE-chuck DEE DING-ding
still as he can be	diam-diam merayap	DEE-uhm DEE-uhm mehr-EYE-yahp
along comes a mosquito	datag seekoor nyamuk	DAH-tung seh-EH-kir NYAH-muhk
HUP!!	HUP!!	HUP!!
He's eaten up.	lalu ditangkup.	LAH-loo DEE-tang-kup

Wood-carvers on Bali Island use sandpaper to smooth their carvings before selling them.

Young Artists

A kid in a family of Indonesian wood-carvers learns the art at an early age. Even toddlers handle the sharp carving tools while a relative watches.

Visual artists, painters, batik makers, weavers, and potters all train their children at a very young age, too. Parents expect that a child will be a skilled artisan by the age of about twelve.

In Flores, Indonesian kids learn how to weave ikat by hand. Each village is known for its own unique style, patterns, and colors. Families also adopt their own ikat pattern.

Sculpture can be found all over Indonesia. Giant statues of epic heroes decorate parks and public buildings. Small stone deities guard the doorways of family temples.

Basket weaving (above right) **is an old art that is still common in Indonesia. These wooden statues** (above) **on Sulawesi Island tell an ancient story of persons long dead.**

Indonesian Fast Food

In Indonesia you can try chicken on a stick from a roadside stand (left). **The fruit in Indonesia is fantastic** (above). **Try the mangoes, bananas, pineapples, coconuts, and papayas.**

All over the islands, vendors push little carts made from cast-off bicycle wheels, old windows, and corrugated tin. They sell *bakso*, *satay* (roasted chicken on a stick), or *gado-gado*. Bakso is the food the tour books tell you never to try, but if you happen to have your own clean bowl, it's definitely worth a taste. For 100 rupiah (about 5 cents), you'll get a steaming bowl of delicious broth, chopped vegetables, noodles, and bakso, little balls of meat.

Janjan, or Indonesian sweet cakes, are a popular snack. Cooks usually make janjan with rice flour that's sweetened with raw sugar from the coconut palm. Some cooks add freshly grated coconut.

Indonesian cooks sometimes color the cakes with natural ingredients. Betel nut makes a beautiful pink, and cinnamon tree leaves make a lovely green. Janjan is especially tasty when the cakes are wrapped in banana leaves and roasted over a wood fire.

Gado-gado

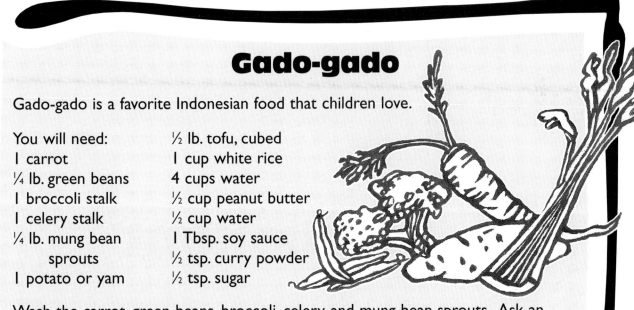

Gado-gado is a favorite Indonesian food that children love.

You will need:
1 carrot	½ lb. tofu, cubed
¼ lb. green beans	1 cup white rice
1 broccoli stalk	4 cups water
1 celery stalk	½ cup peanut butter
¼ lb. mung bean	½ cup water
sprouts	1 Tbsp. soy sauce
1 potato or yam	½ tsp. curry powder
	½ tsp. sugar

Wash the carrot, green beans, broccoli, celery, and mung bean sprouts. Ask an adult to help you cut them into bite-sized pieces. Steam the vegetables a few minutes until tender. Boil the potato or yam in its skin for about twenty minutes or until well cooked. Ask an adult to remove the yam from the pot with tongs. When it is cool, cut it into cubes.

In a pot, bring the rice and water to a boil. Turn the heat down to the lowest possible setting and simmer until the rice is sticky and solid. Cool and use a spoon to break it up into bite-sized pieces. In a big bowl, toss together the steamed vegetables, potato, tofu, and rice. Refrigerate.

To make the peanut sauce, use a fork to combine the peanut butter, water, soy sauce, curry powder, and sugar in a medium bowl. Pour the peanut sauce over the tossed vegetables, rice, and tofu. Enjoy!

An ocean breeze and a blue sky are just what kids need to bring out their kites.

That's **Entertainment**

Looking for something to do? In March fly a kite at a kite festival. Most Indonesian kids like to make their own kites. Kids join clubs that build monster-sized kites. A kite's shape is limited only by one's imagination—birds, bats, boxes, rocket ships, and butterflies are all possibilities. On the day of the festival, the kids who made the huge kites carry them down the streets toward the beach. At the beach, the ocean winds send the kites high in the air.

In Indonesia, rooster fights are legal on religious holidays. If you have a chance to see a rooster fight, don't stand too close. Owners strap

Sepak bola, or soccer, is a favorite sport in Indonesia.

razors to the roosters' legs. Spectators can get hurt when the birds thrash. Spectators bet money on the fights. The owner of the winning chicken takes home cash. The losing chicken makes a tasty dinner.

Cock fighting is a favorite Indonesian pastime. Stay away from the fighting roosters!

Learn a traditional Indonesian dance like these children from the countryside.

Glossary

archipelago: A group of islands.

continent: One of the seven great divisions of land on the globe.

earthquake: The shaking of the ground caused by shifting plates in the earth's crust or by a volcanic eruption.

equator: The imaginary line that circles the globe's middle section halfway between the North Pole and the South Pole.

ethnic group: A large community of people who share a number of social features, such as language, religion, or customs.

extended family: Mothers, fathers, brothers, sisters, grandparents, aunts, uncles, and cousins who live together in one household.

folktale: A story told within a given culture that explains important ideas, such as where an ethnic group came from or how the world began.

rain forest: A dense, green forest that receives large amounts of rain every year. These forests lie near the equator.

tectonic plates: The pieces of land that make up the Earth's crust.

tropical: A region or climate that is frost free, with temperatures high enough to support year-round plant growth.

tsunami: A tidal wave, which is created by undersea earthquakes or volcanic eruptions.

volcano: An opening in the earth's surface through which hot, melted rock and gases are thrown up with explosive force. *Volcano* can also refer to the hill or mountain of ash and rock that builds up around the opening. Volcanoes may be active or dormant. An active volcano can erupt at any time. Dormant volanoes haven't erupted for a long, long time.

A Taste of the Wild

Indonesian kids have been known to munch on deep-fried dragonflies after school. Or snackers might choose a handful of grubs or termites served over rice. Some feast on steaming plates of mice, porcupine, or fruit bat. For something cool and refreshing, folks choose monkey salad. Every bone, tooth, and nail of a monkey is ground to a pulp and mixed with diced ferns, onions, garlic, chilies, and bitter starfruit leaves. Cooks then toss the blend with the monkey's blood before serving.

Pronunciation Guide

Agama Asli	ah-GAH-mah AH-slee
angklung	AHNG-kluhng
archipelago	ahr-keh-peh-leh-GOH
Bahasa	bah-wah-SAH
Bali	BAH-lee
bambu gila	BAHM-boo GEE-lah
bemo	BEH-moh
Bhinneka Tunggal Ika	bih-neh-KAH TOANG-gahl EE-kah
dalang	dah-LAHNG
gamelon joged bumbung	GAH-meh-lahn JOH-gehd BOOM-buhng
id al-Fitr	EED AHL FEE-tree
Indonesia	ihn-doh-NEE-zhah
keluarga adat	keh-loo-AHR-gah ah-DAHT
Krakatoa	krah-kah-TOH-ah
Labuhanbajo	lah-buh-HAHN-bah-joh
Lamaholot	lah-mah-HOH-loht
Larantuka	lah-rahn-TOO-kah
Mahabarata	mah-hah-bah-RAH-tah
Minangkabau	mee-nahng-KAH-bow
Pygmy	PIHG-mee
rafflesia arnoldi	rah-fleh-SEE-ah ahr-NOHL-dee
Ramayana	rah-mah-YAH-nah
rupiah	roo-PEE-ah
Saraswati	sah-RAH SWAH-tee
Sekola Dasar	seh-KOH-lah DAH-sahr
Sekola Menangah Atas	seh-KOH-lah meh-NEH-ngah AH-tahs
Sekola Menengah Pertama	seh-KOH-lah meh-NEH-ngah pehr-TAH-mah
Sumatra	Soo-MAH-trah
wayang kulit	wah-YANG koo-LEET

Further Reading

Berg, Elizabeth. *Festivals of the World: Indonesia*. Milwaukee: Gareth Stevens Publishing, 1997.

Chenevière, Alain. *Pak in Indonesia*. Minneapolis: Lerner Publications Company, 1996.

Cox, David. *Ayu and the Perfect Moon*. London: The Bodley Head, 1984.

Indonesia in Pictures. Minneapolis: Lerner Publications Company, 1995.

Johnson, Sylvia A. *Rice*. Minneapolis: Lerner Publications Company, 1985.

Kimishima, Hisako. *The Princess of the Rice Fields: An Indonesian Folktale*. New York: Walker/Weatherhill, 1970.

Macdonald, Robert. *Islands of the Pacific Rim and Their People*. New York: Thomson Learning, 1994.

Ryan, Patrick. *Indonesia*. Chanhassen, MN: Child's World, 1998.

Metric Conversion Chart

WHEN YOU KNOW:	MULTIPLY BY:	TO FIND:
teaspoon	5.0	milliliters
tablespoon	15.0	milliliters
cup	0.24	liters
inches	2.54	centimeters
feet	0.3048	meters
miles	1.609	kilometers
square miles	2.59	square kilometers
degrees Fahrenheit	5/9 (after subtracting 32)	degrees Celsius

Index